G

CENGAGE Learning

Short Stories for Students, Volume 6

Staff

Editorial: Tim *Akers, Editor.* Donald Akers, Tim Akers, Thomas Bertonneau, Cynthia Bily, Paul Bodine, Carol Dell'Amico, Catherine V. Donaldson, Tom Faulkner, Benjamin Goluboff, Diane Andrews Henningfeld, Rena Korb, Oliver Lovesey, Sarah Madsen Hardy, Jacqueline Perret, Elisabeth Piedmont-Marton, Eric Rapp, *Sketchwriters.* Jeffrey W. Hunter, Maria Job, Daniel Jones, Deborah A. Schmitt, Polly Vedder, Timothy J. White, Kathleen Wilson, *Contributing Editors.* James P. Draper, *Managing Editor.*

Research: Victoria B. Cariappa, *Research Team Manager.* Andrew Malonis, *Research Specialist.*

Permissions: Maria Franklin, *Interim Permissions Manager.* Kimberly Smilay, *Permissions Specialist.* Kelly Quin, *Permissions Associate.* Sandra K. Gore, *Permissions Assistant.*

Production: Mary Beth Trimper, *Production Director*. Evi Seoud, *Assistant Production Manager*. Cindy Range, *Production Assistant*.

Graphic Services: Randy Bassett, *Image Database Supervisor*. Mikal Ansari, Robert Duncan, *Imaging Specialists*. Pamela A. Reed, *Photography Coordinator*.

coordination, expression, arrangement, and classification of information. All rights to this publication will be vigorously defended.

Copyright 1999
The Gale Group
27500 Drake Road
Farmington Hills, MI 48331-3535

This book is printed on acid-free paper that meets the minimum requirements of American National Standard for Information Sciences—Permanence Paper for Printed Library Materials, ANSI Z39.48-1984.

ISBN 0-7876-3606-1
ISSN 1092-7735

Printed in the United States of America
10 9 8 7 6 5 4 3 2

Hills Like White Elephants

Ernest Hemingway 1927

Introduction

First published in *transition* in August of 1927, "Hills Like White Elephants" became an important piece in Hemingway's second collection of short stories, *Men Without Women*. Hemingway wrote the story soon after the publication of his 1926 novel, *The Sun Also Rises,* while living in Paris. *Men Without Women* was well-received, as were Hemingway's other early works. He was embraced by the expatriate literary community in Paris and received strong reviews on his work in the United States and abroad. Although he continued to write novels and stories throughout his career, the early short stories are often considered to be among his finest works. "Hills Like White Elephants," a widely-anthologized and much-discussed story, offers a glimpse at the spare prose and understated dialogue that represents Hemingway's mastery of style.

The story, told nearly in its entirety through dialogue, is a conversation between a young woman and a man waiting for a train in Spain. As they talk, it becomes clear that the young woman is pregnant and that the man wants her to have an abortion. Through their tight, brittle conversation, much is revealed about their personalities. At the same time, much about their relationship remains hidden. At the end of the story it is still unclear as to what decision has or has not been made, or what will happen to these two characters waiting for a train on a platform in Spain.

Author Biography

Ernest Hemingway was born in Oak Park, Illinois, on July 21, 1899, to Clarence and Grace Hemingway. His father was a doctor and his mother a musician who had given up her career to care for the couple's six children.

Hemingway's early life was an upper-middle class, comfortable existence. He and his family spent summers at their cottage in northern Michigan. He graduated from high school and went to work as a reporter, a career he continued on and off for the rest of his life.

The comfortable life ended, however, in 1918, when Hemingway volunteered as a Red Cross ambulance driver to do service on the front lines of World War I in Europe. While in Italy, just before his nineteenth birthday, he was severely wounded while helping to rescue another wounded man. The experiences that Hemingway had in the war and during his recuperation stayed with him for the rest of his life, impacting his work greatly.

After the war, Hemingway returned to his work as a reporter. He married Hadley Richardson in 1921 and the couple moved to Paris. There he developed connections with other expatriate writers, including Ezra Pound and Gertrude Stein, among others. He also met and established a friendship with James Joyce. Throughout this period, he continued to work as a correspondent while launching his own literary career.

In 1926, Hemingway published *The Sun Also Rises,* his first novel, which generated considerable critical attention. The novel firmly established Hemingway as the voice of his generation, which is sometimes referred to as the "lost generation." He continued to meet with success in publishing his short stories. In 1927, he and his first wife divorced and he married Pauline Pfeiffer. In that same year, he published the well-received collection of short stories, *Men Without Women,* a collection that included the short story, "Hills Like White Elephants."

In the years that followed, the Hemingways established a household in Key West, Florida. In 1929, Hemingway's novel *A Farewell to Arms* was published. Hemingway's fame continued to grow, but not only for his literary skill—his "extracurricular" activities placed him squarely in the public eye. He hunted big game in Africa in the 1930s and German submarines in the Caribbean in the 1940s, and after covering the Spanish Civil War as a reporter, he memorialized the Loyalist cause in *For Whom the Bell Tolls* (1940).

By 1940, Hemingway had moved to Cuba and married his third wife, Martha Gellhorn. He subsequently divorced Gellhorn and married Mary Welsh in 1946. In 1952, he published *The Old Man and the Sea,* for which he was awarded the 1953 Pulitzer Prize. In 1954, Hemingway won the Nobel Prize in Literature.

Hemingway's final years were filled with growing physical and mental pain. In 1961, at his home in Ketchum, Idaho, he took his own life with a shotgun blast, ending a decades-long literary career and a life filled with both the highest adventure and the deepest depression. His work continues to generate immense critical and popular interest.

Plot Summary

The story opens with the description of distant hills across a river in Spain. An American and his girlfriend sit outside a train station in the heat. No other details about their relationship are provided at the beginning of the story. They decide to order beer, and the woman who works at the bar brings the drinks to their table. The girl remarks that the distant hills look like white elephants, but the man discounts her remark.

The story continues to unfold through dialogue, and it becomes clear that the girl, Jig, does not understand Spanish while the American does. In addition, it begins to become apparent that the two are having some sort of disagreement. The subject of the disagreement, however, is hidden, until the man says, "It's really an awfully simple operation, Jig. . . . It's not really an operation at all." When Jig fails to respond, the man tries several more times to tell her that the "operation" is all "perfectly natural." His description of the operation implies that Jig is pregnant and he is trying to talk her into having an abortion.

Jig wants reassurance that if she has the operation the American will still love her and that life will go back to the way it was before the pregnancy. However, even as she asks for reassurance, it becomes clear that she does not want to have the abortion. Further, it also becomes clear that she understands that nothing will ever be the same again.

Although the man continues to assert that he does not want her to have the abortion unless she wants to, he obviously does not mean this. Jig stands, and looks out across the valley. She seems to contemplate what is at stake in their relationship and in her life. When she says that they "could have everything," the man agrees. For Jig, "everything" seems to include the baby. For the American, it means carefree life without the baby. Jig finally becomes frustrated with the conversation and asks the man to be quiet. Rather than listen to her, he continues to tell her how she ought to feel, and what she ought to realize. In addition, he continues to tell her that he knows exactly what the operation will be like. Finally, she quietly explodes: "Will you please please please please please please please stop talking?"

The man tries once more, but Jig tells him she will scream. He takes the bags to the other side of the station and quickly has a drink at the bar as he passes through. He observes that many people are "reasonably" waiting for the train, supposedly in contrast to what he sees as unreasonable behavior from Jig. He returns to the table and Jig smiles at him. He asks if she is better, and she replies that she feels fine. The story ends before the train arrives and with little indication of what the final decision will be or what the state of the relationship will be in the future.

The American

The American is one of two characters in Hemingway's story. He sits at a table with a girl at a train station in Spain. Through his conversation, it becomes clear that the girl with him is his lover. Throughout the story, the American tries to convince the girl that she should have an abortion. He tries to make himself sound perfectly reasonable and rational, but as the dialogue continues, it becomes clear that he is both selfish and hypocritical. He says, "You've got to realize. . .that I don't want you to do it if you don't want to. I'm perfectly willing to go through with it if it means anything to you." He does not mean, however, that he wants the girl to have the baby, although he says that he'll "go through with it." By the end of the story, the American has revealed himself to be self-centered and lacking in feeling for the girl, Jig, despite his protestations of love.

The girl

See Jig

Jig

The second character is called "Jig" by the

American; however, Hemingway refers to her as "the girl" throughout the story. This is in contrast to Hemingway's naming of the other character as "the American" or "the man." Jig is a young woman who finds herself pregnant with her lover's child. She and her lover have been traveling in Europe; the labels on their suitcases name the hotels where they have spent nights together. At the time of the story, she is sitting at a table with the American, drinking beer and anise liqueur, waiting for a train. It slowly becomes clear that the man is trying to talk her into aborting the child she carries. Although the subject is never mentioned directly, the pregnancy is at the heart of the conversation. It is not clear what decision Jig reaches by the end of the story, or if she has reached any decision at all. It does seem clear, however, that she is unhappy with both choices in front of her: keep the baby and lose the American, or abort the baby and keep the American. She seems unconvinced that either scenario will develop as the American promises it will.

Media Adaptations

- "Hills Like White Elephants" is one of three short stories filmed as a cable television movie. The other two stories on the film include "The Man in the Brooks Brother Shirt" by Mary McCarthy, and "Dusk Before Fireworks" by Dorothy Parker. The ninety minute film aired on HBO entertainment network in 1990 as *Men and Women.* The video version of the film is titled *Women and Men: Three Tales of Seduction* and is a 1996 Front Row Entertainment production. David Brown and William S. Gilmore are the producers. The film stars Beau Bridges, Melanie Griffith, Elizabeth McGovern, Molly Ringwald, Peter Weller, and James Woods.

As the story closes, Jig asserts that she is "just fine." Under the circumstances, however, it is clear that this is not the case.

Choices and Consequences

"Hills Like White Elephants" presents a couple in the midst of a crisis. Although unmarried, the girl is pregnant and the man who has made her pregnant wants her to have an abortion. His belief is that the choice for abortion will free them to return to the lives they had lived before the pregnancy. He does not want to share the girl with anyone, particularly not a baby. He believes that the consequences of having the baby will lead to the breakup of the relationship.

Jig, however, seems to have a more realistic assessment of the choices and consequences in front of her. She knows that she is the one who must make the choice about the child she carries. Although she asks for reassurance, and wants the man's love, she also knows that the chances of them finding long term happiness are remote, regardless of the decision she makes. For her, the choice to abort or not to abort will, in all likelihood, render the same consequences: life without the American.

Doubt and Ambiguity

The story of Jig and the American is a story of doubt and ambiguity for the American, for Jig, and for the reader. While the American speaks in the language of certainty, he may or may not mean what he says. In addition, he can have little knowledge of what it would mean to the girl to have the abortion he so desperately wants her to have.

Although she seems unconvinced that the abortion is the best plan, Jig nonetheless wants reassurance from the man that she is with that he will stay with her. "And if I do it you'll be happy and things will be like they were and you'll love me?" she asks the man. His reassurances seem to fall flat, however. For Jig, the path ahead is unclear. If she chooses to have the abortion, she may be unhappy with the loss. The American may leave her anyway. She may not survive the operation, in spite of the American's reassurances that it is "perfectly simple." If she chooses not to have the abortion, she may be left alone in Spain, without support, in a country where she does not even speak the language.

Even at the very end of the story, there seems to be no resolution. What does Jig decide? Does she get on the train or not? Does the couple stay together or separate? The clues in the story are sparse, and can be read either way. Thus, the doubt and ambiguity facing the characters are mirrored by the story itself.

Men and Women

In "Hills Like White Elephants," Hemingway explores the way that men and women relate to each other. Hemingway's stories are often heavily masculine, and his protagonists are often patriarchal and sexist. As Peter Messent argues, however, in this story, Hemingway "foregrounds a woman's point of view." The more the American speaks, the more ridiculous he becomes. For example, he tells Jig, "It's really an awfully simple operation, Jig. . . . It's not really an operation at all." Jig does not respond to this statement for several reasons. First, she knows what an abortion is and how it will be performed. It is, after all, her body. In addition, it is not simple: abortions are not legal at this time and place (abortion was not legalized in Spain until 1985), and sometimes women die. Jig knows this, and the man's denial of the complexity of what he is asking the woman to do only serves to highlight his own selfishness.

In addition, throughout the opening part of the story, the American tries to talk Jig into the abortion by telling her how simple it is. He claims superior knowledge and wants her to acquiesce. The moment, however, that she says she will have the abortion because *he* wants her to have it, the man says, "I don't want you to do it if you don't want to. I'm perfectly willing to go through with it if it means anything to you." The use of "it" in this line is revealing: it refers not only to the abortion, but to the baby as well. And although the American wants Jig to have the abortion, he does not want to assume the responsibility for it. Not only must she have the abortion to keep him, she must also agree to the abortion on his terms, as something she wants. In this story, Hemingway suggests that sometimes a man wants to control not only the situation he finds himself in, but also the reactions a woman has to the situation as well.

Style

Setting

In "Hills Like White Elephants" the setting serves both to locate the story in space and time and to function as an important symbol. The story is set in Spain, in the valley of the Ebro River. More immediately, the setting is a railway station "between two lines of rails in the sun." The American and the girl sit at a table. On one side of the station, the land is parched and desolate. A number of critics have noted the similarity between this landscape and that of T. S. Eliot's *The Wasteland*. On the other side of the station, there are trees and grain. By dividing the setting in half, with one side sterile and the other fertile, Hemingway uses the setting to reinforce the division between the couple. They can choose sterility through the abortion, or fertility through the pregnancy. The landscape outside the couple's conversation reflects the inner landscapes of the relationship.

Topics for Further Study

- Read *The Sun Also Rises* and the other stories in *Men Without Women*. How do you characterize the human relationships portrayed by Hemingway in the books? What different kinds of relationships does Hemingway explore?

- Investigate the American expatriate community in Paris during the years 1920 through 1929. Who are the members of the community? What is their relationship to each other? How did their close affiliation affect their writing?

- The Treaty of Versailles ended the hostilities of the First World War. However, many historians argue that the terms of the treaty made the

Second World War inevitable. Investigate the treaty and the years between the wars. Describe the connections between the Treaty of Versailles and movement toward World War II.

- The role and status of women changed dramatically during the years from 1920-1929. Investigate this shift by looking at representations of women in art, music, and literature. What does this investigation reveal about the relationship between the sexes at this time?

- Visit an art gallery, or check out books on art from your library. Examine art produced during the years between 1920 and 1929. How is this work different from the work produced during the last half of the nineteenth century? What might account for the dramatic shifts?

Dialogue

The most striking feature of this story is that it is constructed almost entirely of dialogue. There are only seven short descriptive paragraphs that are not part of the dialogue itself. Further, there is very little action in the story: the girl walks from one side of the station to the other, they drink beer, and the man moves the luggage. By controlling the narrative so tightly, Hemingway forces the reader to participate in the scene almost as an eavesdropper. The reader "hears" the dialogue, but cannot break into the characters' inner thoughts. With so little else present, the weight and the meaning of the story depend on the reader's ability to decipher the cryptic comments the two characters make to each other. Hemingway himself once suggested that a short story is like the tip of an iceberg, the meaning of the story submerged beneath the written text. Certainly in "Hills Like White Elephants," only the smallest portion of the story's subject is apparent, and the reader must guess at the rest.

Lost Generation

The term "Lost Generation" has come to apply to a group of young writers, most born around 1900, who fought in the First World War. As a group, the Lost Generation found that their understanding of life had been severely affected by their experiences during the war. Many of the Lost Generation lived in Europe, notably in Paris, during the post-War period. The term came from a comment that Gertrude Stein made to Hemingway, "You are all a lost generation." Hemingway used the comment as a epigraph in his novel, *The Sun Also Rises*. Other writers included in this group are F. Scott Fitzgerald, Hart Crane, Louis Bromfield, and Malcolm Cowley.

The aimlessness of the characters in "Hills Like White Elephants" is one of the characteristics of the fiction of the Lost Generation. Jig and the Americans are expatriates, moving from place to place to "look at things and try new drinks." They are people who live in hotels, out of luggage, rather than being rooted in one place. The lack of rootedness, then, becomes an important motif in the literature of this generation.

Europe Between the Wars

Hemingway wrote "Hills Like White Elephants" in 1926 while living in Paris. Europe between the First and Second World Wars provided the historical and cultural context for the story. Hemingway was twenty-two, newly married and ready to begin a career as a serious writer when he arrived in Paris in 1921. His experiences as an ambulance driver during World War I continued to affect him, and the sense of alienation and isolation characteristic of modernist writing can be found in the writing he produced during these years.

Europe was in the process of recovering from the war; however, it was a time of political and economic upheaval for most of the nations. Many nations suffered political struggles as right and left wing factions attempted to wrest control of their particular countries. In Italy, for example, strikes, violence, and political unrest led to the 1922 Fascist March on Rome. Mussolini established himself as dictator in that country. In Germany, the heavy reparations called for in the Treaty of Versailles that ended WWI caused economic chaos. The German mark steadily lost ground as the rate of inflation spiraled upward. Germans would rush to buy goods the moment they received cash because the value of their cash would decrease by the end of the day. The other nations of Europe, their countryside scarred and their young men dead or wounded, reeled under a deep and severe recession.

The Lost Generation

In the United States, however, the economy boomed. The stock market reached dizzying heights and the dollar enjoyed an extremely favorable rate of exchange with most European currencies. In addition, many young Americans had been in Europe during the War, allowing them to feel more comfortable in the different cultures. Armed with the strong American dollar and the familiarity with the language and culture, many writers found Paris a very attractive milieu—collectively, these writers became known as the "Lost Generation." According to Michael Reynolds, some six thousand Americans lived in Paris at the end of 1921; by "September 1924, the city's permanent American population was thirty thousand and rising." Hemingway brushed shoulders with many notable writers and literary figures while in Paris, including Ezra Pound, Gertrude Stein, Alice B. Toklas, F. Scott Fitzgerald, and James Joyce, among others.

Hemingway himself popularized the idea of a lost generation through his first novel, *The Sun Also Rises*. In his later memoir of the Paris years, *A Moveable Feast,* Hemingway writes of a conversation he had with the writer Gertrude Stein in which she called all young people who had been in the war "a lost generation." Subsequently,

Hemingway used Stein's comment as one of two epigraphs that open the book. Hemingway, perhaps better than any other writer of his generation, captured the sense of waste and loss and the resulting aimlessness that the War engendered in the young people of his era.

Compare & Contrast

- **1920s:** Post-war American economy roars, fueled by a growing stock market. Credit is easy, and fortunes are made and lost in a day. The culture becomes increasingly consumer-oriented as new technology puts desirable products into the hands of the middle classes.
  1990s: The United States enjoys a period of nearly unprecedented prosperity. Credit is easy, and the stock market spirals upward. The growth of technology has made computers, video games, digital cameras, and cell phones affordable for the middle classes.

- **1920s:** Women finally receive the right to vote in the United States. They use their new-found voting power to make the consumption of alcohol illegal in the United States through a Constitutional Amendment prohibiting the making or sale of alcohol. Women work outside the home, and the "flapper" becomes the symbol for a generation of young women.

1990s: Women hold elected offices, serve on the Unites States Supreme Court, and manage large corporations. Nevertheless, the earning power of women still lags behind that of men. Sexual discrimination and harassment laws protect women from being fired or demoted because of their gender.

- **1920s:** Abortions are illegal in most countries in Europe and in the United States. Nevertheless, many women have abortions, and many die from poorly performed illegal abortions. Because there is no reliable means of birth control, and because of the great social stigma against unmarried mothers, women endanger their own lives rather than endure social censure.

  1990s: Abortions are legal in the United States. In Spain, abortions have been legal since 1985. In the United States, a growing segment of the population believes that abortion is wrong, with some anti-abortion activists turning to violence. Abortion doctors are murdered and abortion clinics subject to bombings and violent demonstrations.

- **1920s:** Modernism, the sense that the old ways of doing things no longer apply, takes hold of art, literature, and culture in Europe and the United States. Artists experiment with new forms and subject matter. In spite of disillusionment with human enterprise, the modernists still believe that art and literature can say something important about reality.

  1990s: Postmodernism grows in response to modernism, now deemed worn out and old. Literature becomes self-reflective and meta-fictional. Reality seems to splinter into ever smaller fragments; truth becomes increasingly contingent.

Social Change

The years between the war were ones of rapid social change. In the United States, the economic boom caused by easy credit and technology allowed people to own products as never before. Middle class people were able to own cars, radios, and telephones.

Social change was reflected in other important ways as well. Perhaps most important, women received the right to vote in 1920 and entered the work force in growing numbers. Women bared their legs, lit up cigarettes, and cut their hair. Such expressions of emancipation threatened traditional male values, and the clash between the genders figured in many of the literary works of the day.

Many writers left the United States, preferring the less restrictive morality of Europe. Disillusioned with civilized society, alienated from traditional values, and shell-shocked from a brutal War, these writers experimented with literary form, content, and style.

Critical Overview

Hemingway's "Hills Like White Elephants" first appeared in the magazine *transition* in August, 1927, and within a few months appeared again in the collection *Men Without Women. The Sun Also Rises,* Hemingway's 1926 novel of life in Paris and Pamplona, had already secured the author's reputation as the spokesperson for his generation. *Men Without Women* further solidified critical approval of his early work. "Hills Like White Elephants" was singled out for special attention from reviewers. For example, Dorothy Parker, enamored with Hemingway and his prose, called the story in an early review "delicate and tragic." She further added, "I do not know where a greater collection of stories can be found."

Virginia Woolf, on the other hand, did not seem appreciate Hemingway or his prose. Her review, contemporary with the publication of the story, was filled with what could be termed "left-handed compliments." For example, she wrote, "There are . . . many stories which, if life were longer, one would wish to read again. Most of them indeed are so competent, so efficient, and so bare of superfluity that one wonders why they do not make a deeper dent in the mind than they do." She criticized Hemingway for "excessive" dialogue and "lack of proportion."

A final contemporary reviewer, Cyril

Connolly, offered a more balanced critique of *Men Without Women*. He wrote that the volume "is a collection of grim little stories told in admirable colloquial dialogue with no point, no moral and no ornamentation." Although he called Hemingway's work "irritating," he also found the stories "readable and full of. . . power and freshness."

In the years after the initial publication of the story, an increasing number of critics have offered readings of "Hills Like White Elephants." Indeed, as the story began to appear ever more frequently in anthologies of short stories and American literature textbooks, it also generated many critical articles. Criticism of the story most generally focuses on structural issues, such as the use of dialogue and/or figurative language; examines the sources, analogues, and biographical material used in the story; or discusses Hemingway's construction of gender and language.

Robert Paul Lamb, for example, has studied Hemingway's role in the development of twentieth-century literary dialogue. He argues that in "Hills Like White Elephants," Hemingway "blurred the line between fiction and drama, allowing dialogue an unprecedented constructive role in a story's composition." He demonstrates the way that the dialogue simultaneously reveals and hides the subject of the story.

Other critics such as Howard L. Hannum concentrate on the symbolism of the story, exploring the many meanings of the term "white elephant" and the contrast between the fertility and sterility of each side of the railway station. He also noted the story's connection to T. S. Eliot's *The Waste Land* in his discussion.

An important way of reading the story for many critics has been to examine gender and communication. Pamela Smiley, for example, in a 1990 article, discusses the story in terms of gender marked language, basing her analysis on the gender communication theory of Deborah Tannen. Peter Messent includes a chapter called "Gender Role and Sexuality" in his book-length study of Hemingway. He argues that "Hemingway's texts show divided attitudes to matters of sexual politics." Further, Messent writes, while many of Hemingway's stories privilege the male protagonists, "Hills Like White Elephants" is a story in which "'women's sensibilities' are certainly not ignored but rather highlighted in an extremely sensitive manner." Messent points out that it may be for this reason that the story has become more frequently anthologized in recent years. Finally, critic Stanley Renner in a 1995 article argues that a close analysis of the language reveals that the story's ending is not as ambiguous as most readers have thought. He believes that Jig's final words reveal that she has decided to keep the baby. For Renner, the story "side[s] with its female character's values" and "understands and sensitively dramatizes her struggle to take charge of her own arena, to have a say about the direction of her own life."

In addition to this sampling of critical approaches, many other critics have undertaken readings of the story. Such variety and diversity in approach suggest that "Hills Like White Elephants" is a rich and open story, one that will continue to engender multiple readings from its many readers.

What Do I Read Next?

- *The Sun Also Rises* (1926) is a semi-autobiographical account of Hemingway's post-World War I experience as an expatriate. The well-received novel earned Hemingway the title of spokesperson for his generation.

- *Where I'm Calling From: New and Selected Stories,* (1988) is a collection by short story writer Raymond Carver. Most critics agree that Carver's style was influenced by Hemingway's early stories.

- Michael Reynolds's *Hemingway: The Paris Years* (1989) is a careful examination of Hemingway's expatriate period in Paris as a member of the "Lost Generation." The time period covered includes the years when Hemingway wrote and published "Hills Like White Elephants."

- *A Moveable Feast* (1964) is Hemingway's memoir of his years as a young writer in Paris. Hemingway worked on the manuscript during 1957 and 1958, and the volume was published after his death in 1961.

Sources

Connolly, Cyril. A review of *Men Without Women.* *New Statesman,* November 26, 1927, p. 208.

Hannum, Howard L. "'Jig Jig to dirty ears': White Elephants to Let." *The Hemingway Review,* Vol. 11, No. 1, Fall, 1991, pp. 46-54.

Hollander, John. "Hemingway's Extraordinary Reality." *Ernest Hemingway,* edited and with an introduction by Harold Bloom, New York: Chelsea House Publishers, 1985, pp. 211-6.

Lamb, Robert Paul. "Hemingway and the Creation of Twentieth Century Dialogue." *Twentieth Century Literature,* Vol. 42, Winter, 1996, pp. 453-80.

Messent, Peter. *Ernest Hemingway,* New York: St. Martin's Press, 1992, pp. 90-92.

Parker, Dorothy. A review of *Men Without Women.* *New Yorker,* October 29, 1927, pp. 92-4.

Renner, Stanley. "Moving to the Girl's Side of 'Hills Like White Elephants'." *The Hemingway Review,* Vol. 15, No. 1, Fall, 1995, pp. 27-41.

Reynolds, Michael. *Hemingway: The Paris Years,* Oxford: Basil Blackwell, 1989.

Smiley, Pamela. "Gender-Linked Miscommunication in 'Hills Like White Elephants'." In *New Critical Approaches to the Short Stories of Ernest Hemingway,* edited by Jackson J. Benson, Duke University Press, 1990, pp. 288-99.

Smith, Paul. "Introduction: Hemingway and the Practical Reader." In *New Essays on Hemingway's Short Fiction,* Cambridge University Press, 1998, pp. 1-18.

Stampfl, Barry. "Similies as Thematic Clues in Three Hemingway Short Stories." *The Hemingway Review,* Vol. 10, No. 2, Spring 1991, pp. 30-8.

Woolf, Virginia. A review of *Men Without Women. New York Herald Tribune Books,* October 9, 1927, pp. 1, 8.

Further Reading

Meyers, Jeffrey, editor. *Hemingway: The Critical Heritage,* London: Routledge and Kegan Paul, 1982.

> Contains many important contemporary reviews of Hemingway's books, including reviews of *Men Without Women* by Virginia Woolf, Dorothy Parker, and Edmund Wilson, among others.

Reynolds, Michael. *The Young Hemingway,* Oxford: Blackwell, 1986.

> A thorough and readable biography of Hemingway's early days by a notable Hemingway biographer.

Rovit, Earl, and Gerry Brenner. *Ernest Hemingway,* Boston: Twayne, 1986.

> An excellent introduction to Hemingway studies. Includes biographical material, criticism of many of Hemingway's works, and a useful bibliography.

Smith, Paul, editor. *New Essays on Hemingway's Short Fiction,* Cambridge University Press, 1998.

> A collection of recent critical essays on Hemingway's short stories. Contains a useful introduction by

editor Paul Smith, "Hemingway and the Practical Reader."

Wagner, Linda W., editor. *Ernest Hemingway: Six Decades of Criticism,* Michigan State University Press, 1987.

A collection of important reviews and critical articles on Hemingway, spanning his entire career.

Ingram Content Group UK Ltd.
Milton Keynes UK
UKHW020654250523
422339UK00013B/235

9 781375 381246